STEWARDSHIP
MINISTRIES

ABOUT THE AUTHOR

Jay Link has a diverse background academically and professionally. He began his professional career in the preaching ministry and while preaching also earned a Master of Divinity degree in Biblical Theology. He eventually left the preaching ministry and went into the financial services industry where he built a successful practice ministering to affluent Christian families. After creating a successful model, he eventually began training other professionals how to develop master stewardship plans for their clients.

He then launched Stewardship Ministries to provide a wide array of life stewardship resources that would be useful and challenging for Christians regardless of their economic status. Over the past few years, Jay has developed a substantial number of small group video modules for Pastors, adults, high school and junior high students as well as two modules for elementary age children all focused on understanding and practicing the principles of life stewardship in every area of their lives. The most common response heard from those who participate in these studies is "life transforming" regardless of whether the participants are mature believers or brand new Christians.

BEGINNING YOUR LIFE STEWARDSHIP JOURNEY

Table of Contents

INTRODUCTION

My goal for you in reading this book is not that after reading it you will *know more*, but that after reading it you will start *living differently*. The content of this short book has the power to totally transform absolutely every area of your life if you will apply its simple, yet powerful, truths and principles of life stewardship.

This book may very likely be one of the most radical books you will ever read. This book is not for the believer who is content with where they are. It is for the believer who knows there is more, much more, to their walk with the King of Kings than they are presently experiencing. It is for those who are looking for, maybe even longing for, a path that will enable them to "break through" to new levels of transformational living empowering them to become a "light on a hill" in the midst of the darkness – allowing the world to see Christ in the flesh, in your flesh.

This book will likely take you less than an hour to read. But, if you are like me, it is going to take you the rest of your life to successfully apply.

What you are about to read is just the beginning of the life stewardship journey. It is my hope and prayer that it will open your eyes, light your fire, enliven your spirit and embolden your resolve to be all in for the One who has called us to follow Him!

Jay Link

CHAPTER ONE

What Is My Relationship to My Stuff?

This is clearly the most foundational question we must answer if we are going to make any progress in our attitudes, perspectives, and decisions in relation to material things—particularly material wealth. If we cannot answer this question with clarity and confidence, we will find ourselves—in spite of our financial successes—underachieving in our lives. If you think of this question as a stool with three legs upon which the answer is balanced, you will be able to better envision the truth about your stuff.

Leg #1

The first "leg" of this stool is the fact that God owns everything because He created everything. King David tells us in Psalm 24:1, "The earth is the Lord's and all it contains, the world, and those who dwell in it." He goes on to add in Psalm 50:10-12,

> *Every animal in the forest belongs to me, and so do the cattle on a thousand hills.*
> *I know all the birds in the mountains,*
> *and every wild creature is in my care.*
> *If I were hungry, I wouldn't tell you,*
> *because I own the world and everything in it.*

Not only did God create everything that exists, He used all of His own materials to build it. So He truly is the only One who can claim to own anything.

If we build something, we may claim it is ours, but if we use someone else's materials to build it, then the owner of those materials can lay some claim to it as well. But in God's case, He not only dreamed it all up, He used His own creative materials to build it.

Leg #2

The second "leg" of this stool is the fact that not only did God create us, but He also redeemed us from slavery to the prince of this world through the death of His son, Jesus Christ. Paul tells us in Titus 2:13b-14, "Christ Jesus, who gave Himself for us to redeem us from every lawless deed, and to purify for Himself a people for His own possession, zealous for good deeds."

This word redeem that Paul uses here is no longer commonly used in our culture today. When I was a young boy it was used often. I remember going to the grocery store with my mother. At the checkout counter, she would be given a certain number of S&H Green Stamps depending on how large her grocery purchase was. The reason I remember this so well is because I was charged with the task of licking those "tasty" little stamps and then putting them into the books.

My mother had a catalog filled with all kinds of products—everything from small kitchen appliances to a car. I was hoping my mother was not saving stamps for the car because it was several thousand Green Stamp books. I could see my tongue being forever stuck to the roof of my mouth from licking that many stamps! What made the Green Stamp catalog so unusual was that instead of having prices for each item, it had the number of S&H Green Stamp books needed. A hand mixer might be four and a half books and a television 120 books. Do you remember the name of the place where you went to get these products? It was called the Redemption Center. It was the place where you would take your Green Stamp books to redeem the item you wanted. In other words, you traded in your stamp books for something you wanted to own.

This is what God did with Jesus. God was willing to redeem us by offering the blood of His own Son, so He could again own us—"a people for His own possession." You see, God owns Christians twice—once because He made us and the second time because He bought us back after we were lost.

One last thought on this leg: What was the reason Paul gave in Titus 2:14 for why God was willing to redeem us? It was so we could be "zealous for good deeds." Keep that thought in mind as we will be discussing this later in the book.

Leg #3

The final "leg" is the fact that we own nothing. We are called by God to be stewards, carrying out the Owner's wishes for His property. It is at this point that we need to come to grips with the terribly misused and abused concept of stewardship.

Before I focus on what stewardship does mean, let me tell you what it does not mean. Churches routinely use the term stewardship to refer to their capital campaigns. These campaigns are simply fundraisers used to get church members to give. But since "fundraiser" has such a negative connotation, they substitute (incorrectly) the seemingly nobler phrase "stewardship drive."

You will often hear churches and pastors use stewardship as a synonym for tithing. I have seen in many church papers and bulletins the term stewardship used as a heading to report the weekly offerings and attendance. All of these uses that link stewardship to giving and tithing are inadequate at best—and entirely wrong at worst.

By definition, a steward is "a person who manages another's property or financial affairs; one who administers anything as the agent of another or others, a manager." So, for us to be "stewards for God," we must acknowledge that all we are and all we have possession of belongs to Him. We are charged with managing His property according to His wishes.

You can see that stewardship is not at all a synonym for tithing and fundraising; it is actually the opposite. Tithing has to do with what you give; stewardship has to do with what you keep. In other words, it is about how you manage everything that you have been entrusted to oversee. What most people miss is that stewardship is more about how you manage what is left over after you give than it is about what you give.

The radical, biblical concept of stewardship is easy enough to understand intellectually. However, it is anything but easy to consistently apply and live out. So what is your relationship to your stuff? You are not the owner; you are merely the caretaker of somebody else's property. And it is your job to manage all of it according to the Owner's wishes. Now, that really changes the game, does it not?

FOOD FOR THOUGHT

1. When you consider yourself in the role of "manager" rather than "owner," how does this change how you view your stuff?

2. Take a couple of minutes and make a list of all that you own (no values, just descriptions). After reading Psalm 24:1 and Psalm 50:10-12, do you think your balance sheet should look differently – or possibly be blank – because you own nothing?

3. What do you think would be your biggest personal struggle if you were to completely relinquish ownership of everything in your life?

Keeping The Heart Of God
At The Heart Of Living

I can think of no better way to define what stewardship really is than with this phrase—keeping the heart of God at the heart of living. Stewardship is all about carrying out the wishes of the Owner. The Owner is God and we are merely the caretakers of His property. Psalm 24:1 states it clearly, "The earth is the Lord's and all it contains, the world and all who live in it." I think this encompasses everything we will ever get our hands on in this lifetime.

This concept of stewardship is critically important, yet so often misunderstood. Even those who intellectually acknowledge that God owns everything do not functionally live as though He does. Let me illustrate my point by asking you to choose which one of the three questions below is the question we should be asking in regards to our material possessions.

1. What do I want to do with all my possessions?

2. What do I want to do with God's possessions?

3. What does God want me to do with His possessions?

No doubt you chose #3 as the proper question. In about thirty years of asking this question, every believer chooses #3. Intellectually, everyone is able to get this part of it. But practically speaking, we live as though

#2 was the right question. We are more than happy to acknowledge that it all belongs to God, but when it comes to making decisions about what to do with what we oversee, we seldom, if ever, seek direction from the Owner.

Let me offer a few simple questions that should demonstrate just how true this is.

- When you bought your last car, did you ask God if this is the car He wanted you to buy with His money?

- When your money manager proposed an investment portfolio for you, did you go to the Lord and ask Him if these were the places He wanted His money invested?

- The last time you went shopping for clothes, did you ask your Father if these were the clothes He wanted you to wear?

- Did we check with God to see if He wanted us to over-indulge His dwelling place with that last meal?

I hope you see my point. We are all routinely guilty of intellectually acknowledging that God owns everything, while we live, spend, and invest like it is all our own. The cornerstone of stewardship is full acknowledgment and consistent practice of allowing God to direct what He wants done with what He has entrusted us to manage.

I have recently been struck quite seriously with the reality that all our sin, at its core, is the result of personal selfishness. I would encourage you to ponder this yourself for a moment. As I have mulled this idea over and over in my mind, I have yet to find any exception. The truth is: we are our own worst enemies. We are continually getting in the way of God's best because we are so consumed with our desires, our rights, our dreams, our passions, and our way that we continually fall into sins of either commission (doing the wrong thing) or omission (not doing the right thing). Think about it. Why do we lie? Why do we cheat? Why do we steal? Why are we afraid? Why do we hate? Why do we commit adultery? Why do we lose our temper? Why do we become addicted to drugs, work, and entertainment? Why do we covet what others have? Why do we wear "masks" around others? Why do we not want to submit to God? I could go on and on, but it always circles back around to self. As the cartoon character Pogo confessed, "We have met the enemy and he is us."

The reason I am making this point is to say that our practical rejection of a life of devoted stewardship is just another example of how self gets in the way of God's best for us. We want to be in charge. We want to make the decisions. We want to "pull the trigger" and get things done. In ignoring the reality that we are nothing more than mere low-level managers who are expected to meticulously carry out the wishes of the all-loving and all-powerful Owner, our personal will, wishes, choices, and decisions prove to be categorically irrelevant to the discussion.

Someone once noted that at the center of SIN is the letter "I." We will always find "I"—self, ego, always looking out for number one—at the center of our sin.

- This is why Jesus said that if we really want to live, we must first die to self. "For whoever wants to save his life will lose it, but whoever loses his life for me will find it" (Matthew 16:25 niv).

- If you want to be first, you must let everyone else go ahead of you. As the scripture says, "The last will be first, and the first last" (Matthew 20:16 esv).

- If you want to be really free, you must submit to slavery. "Whoever wants to become great among you must be your servant, and whoever wants to be first must be your slave" (Matthew 20:26-27 niv).

- If you want to be great, you must strive to make everyone else greater than yourself. "Do nothing out of selfish ambition or vain conceit, but in humility consider others better than yourselves" (Philippians 2:3 niv, see also Luke 9:48).

It is all about death to self.

The reason stewardship is so challenging to practice is that we must get self out of the way. As long as we are fallen creatures with a fallen nature, we will have to wrestle daily with the lingering ghosts of our own selfishness until we someday finally shed this "dirt body" and move on to better things. In the mean time, we must resist with every ounce of our being the temptation to inappropriately assume the throne and play little gods over stuff that does not even belong to us.

FOOD FOR THOUGHT

1. How have you seen an intellectual disconnect between knowing that question #3 is the right question and how you are currently living and handling your possessions?

2. How does your own sinfulness/selfishness cause you to "inappropriately assume the throne and play little gods over stuff that does not even belong to you"?

3. What would be different in your life starting tomorrow if you were to return everything you possess back to God, the owner?

CHAPTER TWO

The One Question that Changes Everything

I like it when someone "cuts to the chase" giving me the bottom line of what they want to say without including all the details. I am often guilty of helping people finish their sentences so they can more quickly get to the point. I assume some of you might be like that too. So, allow me to boil the quite massive subject of stewardship down to one simple, yet incredibly profound and life-changing question. The question may be simple to ask, it is anything but simple to answer.

Before I give you the question, let me first highlight one irrefutable truth that we need to acknowledge. This one truth is that God owns everything that exists, including you and me.

Just one of the many passages that confirm God's ownership of everything is found in Job 41:11 where God is forcefully questioning Job, "Who has given to Me that I should repay him? Whatever is under the whole heaven is Mine." God actually owns us believers in a second way as Paul points out in Titus 2:14, "Christ Jesus; who gave Himself for us, that He might redeem us from every lawless deed and purify for Himself a people for His own possession…." Paul is emphasizing that God is the owner and we are the owned. So, when we sit down to prepare a balance sheet of all we own, the list should be very short. In fact, the page should be blank. We own nothing, period. It is all His.

Accepting this foundational truth properly prepares us to ask the one question that changes everything. Unfortunately, it is not a question we can ask once, answer once and then move on. It is a question we must ask routinely, daily, sometimes even hourly. Have I adequately piqued your interest as to what this profound and life-changing stewardship question is?

Here it is - simple to ask, but difficult to answer. "God, what do You want me to do with all that You have entrusted to me?" We all seem to be more than willing to acknowledge that God owns everything, but we still seem to continue making all the decisions regarding what we do with what we have. The ultimate objective of our stewardship (management) of God's property is to do with it what He (the Owner) wants us (the managers) to do with it. What we want to do with our stuff is frankly irrelevant.

Does this idea seem restrictive to you – that you don't get to make any decisions about what will be done with all that you possess? At first blush, it can feel that way. But allow me to put this "you mean I'm not in charge" issue into a broader context.

The Perfect Role Model

Jesus, the one we are all attempting to imitate had no qualms about completely yielding His will to the will of His Father while He was temporarily dwelling on this planet He created. He repeatedly informed people Who was in charge of His life. In John 12:49 He notes the source of all that He says, "For I did not speak on My own initiative, but the Father Himself who sent Me has given Me a commandment as to what to say and what to speak." In John 8:28 He adds all His actions to this, "...I do nothing on My own initiative." In other words, everything that Jesus said and everything that He did was directed by the Father. He was not saying or doing anything apart from His Father's directions.

What about when this God-man and His Father disagreed on a plan of action – for example when Jesus had second thoughts about His pending trip to the cross? Jesus willingly yielded His own will to His Father's. He prayed, "My Father, if it is possible, may this cup be taken from Me. Yet not as I will, but as You will" (Matthew 26:39). God was in charge of every aspect of Jesus' life.

There is an unavoidable question that inevitably emerges from all this. If Jesus willingly yielded all of His words, His actions and even His very life to the will of the Father, dare we be so arrogant or rebellious to make unilateral decisions about our lives and possessions without first consulting with the Father? In other words, are we personally emulating Jesus' submission statement in John 5:30, "I can do nothing on My own initiative...because I do not seek My own will, but the will of Him who sent Me"?

As the game show hosts would always say, "But wait, there's more!" Jesus not only models this for us, He also gives us very direct instruction on how we ought to be handling our Father's property.

As Jesus taught His disciples to pray in His Model Prayer on the Sermon on the Mount, He told them to pray, "Your kingdom come. Your will be done, on earth as it is in heaven" (Matthew 6:10). We have no problem with God's will being done in heaven; the problem is down here on earth, isn't it? The solution to this heaven on earth challenge is for us to willingly allow God's will to rule in how we manage our personal lives and what we do with the temporary possessions we watch over down here. In so doing, each believer will allow God's Kingdom to come and His will to be done in his or her little part of earth as it is in heaven.

Can You Imagine?

Can you imagine what would happen to this world if God's people were to make all their time fully available for His use? What about if they devoted all their talents and whatever was needed of their material resources to carry out God's purposes? What would happen if they cared for their bodies like the sacred temple that it really is? What if they saw their employment and careers as an extension of God's calling on their lives and a fulfillment of their God-given purpose? What would happen if all their energies were clearly focused on knowing and following their Owner's agenda and being the most obedient and effective managers possible of what He has entrusted to them?

Can you imagine how your personal life would change if each morning as you rose from your bed, you were to genuinely and humbly pray, "Okay, Lord, all that I am and all that I have are at your disposal today. What are your plans for me and my stuff today? Not my will, but Thy will be done this day."

We know those blessed words that we all long to hear from the Lord when we stand before Him, "Well done..." (Matthew 25:21, 23 nasb). I must confess that I have so focused on these two words that until recently I have never really pondered the two adjectives that describe the "slave" who will hear these words. The "well done" commendation goes to the "slave" who is "good and faithful."

He doesn't say, "Well done, efficient and productive slave." He doesn't say, "Well done, doer of great deeds slave." He doesn't say, "Well done, generous and sacrificial slave." He uses two simple adjectives – good and faithful. As I first considered these words, I rather felt like the bar that Jesus had set in this statement was actually far lower than I had previous understood.

However, as I meditated on these two words further, I began to realize that He may have actually set the bar much higher than I thought. He will someday say well done to his slaves because of what they are (good and faithful) and not because of what they may have done – our being is just as important as our doing. And for slaves who tend to be more focused on the doing than on the being, this revelation can be quite a sobering realization.

I can think of no better way for us to someday hear, "Well done, good and faithful slave" from our Father than for us to be continually asking Him this one question, "God, what do You want me to do with what You have entrusted to me?" And as He reveals His plans for us and for the stuff He has put under our care and management, we need to obediently carry out those plans as faithfully and as well as we can. We need to be good and faithful slaves regardless of how much or how little we have been entrusted with or how much or how little we ultimately accomplish for Him.

I hope you can now see why this one "simple" question, "God, what do You want me to do with what You have entrusted to me," really does change everything. When we faithfully discern and follow His directives, we will in a very real and a very tangible way allow God's Kingdom to come and God's will to be done on earth as it is in heaven!

FOOD FOR THOUGHT

1. What areas of your life right now do you think might be most difficult for you to totally surrender to the will of our Father? Why?

2. What most amazes you about Jesus' absolute surrender to His Father – even to every single word He spoke?

3. How do you think asking this one question, "God, what do You want me to do today with what You have entrusted to me" will change your life if you were to earnestly and sincerely pray it each morning?

CHAPTER THREE

The Defining Characteristics of a Good and Faithful Steward

Tragic as it is, the concept of stewardship is so poorly taught and so poorly practiced among followers of Jesus that it is necessary to provide a clear description of how a good and faithful steward should live. The life of an obedient steward possesses three dominant life-characteristics. As we consider each of these characteristics, may it enable us to better assess how well we are personally living the life of a good and faithful steward.

A Good and Faithful Steward Lives an Examined Life

This practice of living a life of regular self-examination is often referenced in the Bible. In II Corinthians 13:5 Paul told the believers in Corinth, "Examine yourselves to see whether you are in the faith; test yourselves..." He also tells them in I Corinthians 11:28 that, "A man ought to examine himself before he eats of the bread and drinks of the cup (communion)." Even Jeremiah exhorts his people in Lamentations 3:40, "Let us test and examine our ways."

There is nothing more appropriate for a faithful manager of someone else's resources than to routinely examine how effectively he is carrying out his responsibilities. A steward will continually examine his behavior, his motives, his thoughts, his attitudes, the direction of his life and how well he is imitating the life of Jesus.

Unfortunately, we often only examine our lives when something is going wrong or we face some significant crisis. In the midst of that trial, we finally pause to take stock of our lives to determine what might have caused this difficult situation. Crisis examination is certainly better than no examination at all, but may I suggest that a good and faithful steward will be doing routine self-examination as part of his daily life.

I have been told by more than one pilot that a plane when in the air is off course about 95% of the time due to wind currents, barometric pressure, etc. Because of this, the pilot must be vigilant in making continual minor course corrections to bring the plane back on course. If he does not, he will find, after several hours of flying that his plane is actually hundreds of miles off course.

The good and faithful steward is like the attentive pilot in flight – continually examining the course of his or her life to determine if it is still following the flight pattern that has been set by the "Tower." The steward will routinely make whatever midcourse corrections to his life that are needed regardless of how subtle or how dramatic they need to be. He recognizes that the gravitational pull of this world and the unpredictable winds of temptation can very quickly get him off course.

Socrates correctly concluded, "The unexamined life is not worth living."

So, would the word examined describe your life?

A Good and Faithful Steward Lives a Controlled Life

Living a controlled life is a foundational characteristic of a good and faithful steward. Self-control is one of the fruits of the Spirit (Galatians

5:23). Paul repeats several times in his letter to Titus that believers are to live a controlled life. Elders are to have their lives under control (Titus 1:8). Older men are to be self-controlled (Titus 2:2). Young men and women are to be self-controlled as well (Titus 2:5-6).

Paul uses the discipline and self-control of an athlete in training to illustrate the controlled life of a steward (I Corinthians 9:25). Just two verses later he applies self-control to himself when he says, "But I discipline my body and keep it under control…"

I think Solomon makes this point best when he says in Proverbs 25:28, "A man without self-control is like a city broken into and left without walls." There is nothing to contain him and he lives a life that is out of control in one or more ways.

We all know people who lack self-control. They cannot control their tempers. They cannot control their appetites. They cannot control their emotions. They cannot control their tongues. They cannot control their sex drives. They cannot control their spending. In one or more ways they are lacking self-control. They are "like a city broken into and left without walls."

The good and faithful steward, to the contrary, is constantly restraining and retraining his natural impulses to keep all of these fleshly desires (both good and bad) under control. He is diligently working day-by-day and often minute-by-minute to keep his head in the game and not allow "the desires of the flesh and the desires of the eyes and pride in possessions…" (I John 2:16) to break down the walls of self-control that is a defining characteristic of a good and faithful steward.

John Milton said well, "He who reins within himself and rules passions, desires and fears is more than a king." The steward who is in control will be both useful and effective in obediently serving his Master. So, would the word controlled describe your life?

A Good and Faithful Steward Lives a Sacrificial Life

The third characteristic that will always be commonly seen in the life of a good and faithful steward is sacrifice. We simply cannot be good and faithful stewards if sacrifice is not a part of our lives.

Paul calls us to be "living sacrifices" (Romans 12:1). Jesus challenges every steward that if he wants to follow Him, "let him deny himself and take up his cross daily and follow me" (Luke 9:23). The cross in Jesus' day was used for only one purpose, to kill someone. So the imagery He is giving us is quite dramatic. He is not calling us to a one-time sacrificial death for "the cause." The sacrifice He is describing here is to be a daily sacrifice. Each day, we are to put to death our wishes, our desires, our agenda, our comforts, our free time and our hopes for the greater good of the Kingdom and the world we seek to win.

In his book The Kingdom and the Cross, James Bryan Smith suggests that, "If our God is self-sacrificing and seeks to bless others who have done nothing to merit it, then we should be people who are self-sacrificing and who bless others who have not earned it."

There is no more powerful demonstration of a good and faithful steward than when he willingly and sacrificially gives to others without any consideration of their worthiness to receive his gift.

Regardless of how great or small the need or opportunity, he gladly sacrifices whatever he currently manages for the good of others.

John gives us the ultimate extent to which we must be willing to live a sacrificial life. He said in I John 3:16, "By this we know love, that He laid down His life for us, and we ought to lay down our lives for the brothers."

If sacrificing our lives is the maximum sacrifice we might be called to make as a steward, it seems to put into a clear context the modest sacrifices we make when we give some of the money, or the time or the talents we have been given to manage to help others.
So, would the word sacrificial describe your life?

If we want to be identified as a good and faithful steward and someday hear those wonderful words, "Well done," we must (1) routinely examine ourselves to be sure that our lives are on the right course that has been set by our Master. (2) We need to be vigilant that we control our appetites and impulses to ensure that they do not end up controlling us. (3) We need to be regularly and generously sacrificing what we have been entrusted with in hopes of bringing a little bit of heaven to those who are here on earth. Living the life of a good and faithful steward is a tremendous challenge. Are you up to the challenge?

FOOD FOR THOUGHT

1. Which of these three areas of life stewardship (the examined life, the controlled life, or the sacrificial life) do you personally most struggle with? Why?

2. When do you most often find yourself willing and desiring to carefully examine your life? Are you more of a routine self-examination person or a life-crisis examination person? How does taking time to do some self-examination help you in your walk with the Lord?

3. What would be the hardest material thing for you to let go of (sacrifice), if the Lord were to call you to release it?

CHAPTER FOUR

Are You Living Your Life on Purpose or by Accident?

People have often asked me what I mean when I encourage people to plan their lives on purpose. My answer is simple. You can choose to live your life one of two ways: you can either live your life on purpose, or you can live your life by accident. In other words, you can plan your life and live your plan, or you can simply let the flow of life events and circumstances sweep you down the river of time taking you wherever it will. The latter, sadly, is the way most people live their lives—by accident. The former is how God created us to live—on purpose. (You can see this in passages like Ephesians 5:15-16 and Psalm 90:12.)

Some might claim that there is something unspiritual about making plans, but for those of us who do, we are in good company. God made plans. (See Hebrews 11:40a, Jeremiah 29:11, Ephesians 1:11.) Paul made plans. (See 2 Corinthians 1:15-17, Romans 15:24.) And we are encouraged to make plans. (See Proverbs 16:3, 20:18, 21:5.)

Unfortunately, when it comes to building one's financial "empire" we can often find ourselves doing it without any real divine purpose behind it. Successful people continue to build up their "pile of stuff" because they have become exceedingly good at what they do. They also find great emotional enjoyment and personal satisfaction in building, so they keep on building without ever giving much thought to where it will end up.

However, I think there is a foundational question that we, as believers, need to ask ourselves, "What is my purpose for continuing to build my financial empire when my pile of stuff is already higher than I will ever need it to be?" Jesus tells us plainly that accumulating excess material possessions as a sole end in itself is entirely futile. Jesus states, "For what will it profit a man if he gains the whole world and forfeits his soul?" (Matthew 16:26). For those who do this are like the rich farmer who planned to tear down his smaller barns and build bigger barns to hold his surplus wealth. Remember, Jesus called him a fool.

There is no greater example of the utter folly of building without a purpose than the story of Sarah Winchester. Sarah was the wife of William Winchester, the only son of Oliver Winchester, the founder and owner of the Winchester Repeating Arms Company. Sarah and William had a daughter who died shortly after birth in 1866. This was followed by the death of her father-in-law (in 1880) and then her husband just a few months later (in 1881), leaving her with a fifty percent ownership in the company and an income of $1,000 a day (about $21,000 a day in current dollars).

Sarah believed that her family was under some kind of a curse and consulted a medium to determine what she should do. The medium told her that her family was indeed cursed by the spirits of all the people that the Winchester rifle had killed. She should move out west and build a house for herself and all the tormented spirits who suffered because of her family. The medium also told her that if construction on this house were to ever cease, she would immediately die.

In 1884 Sarah moved to California and began one of the most bizarre building stories in American history. She began spending her $20 million inheritance and regular income to buy and begin renovating an eight-room farmhouse in what is now San Jose, California. From that day forward construction continued nonstop, twenty-four hours a day, seven days a week until Sarah's death at age eighty-three—a total of thirty-eight years. She kept no less than twenty-two carpenters busy continuously. The sounds of hammers and saws could be heard throughout the day and night for almost four decades.

At its zenith, this seven story house contained 160 rooms, forty bedrooms, forty-seven fireplaces, seventeen chimneys, and 10,000 windowpanes. What made Sarah's lifetime building project so bizarre was that it had no discernable architectural purpose or plan behind it. Closet doors opened to solid walls. Windows were in the floor. Stairways led to nowhere. Railings were installed upside down. Drawers were only one inch deep. Trapdoors were everywhere. Blind chimneys stopped short of the ceiling. There were double-back hallways. Doors opened to steep drops to the lawn below. Many of the bathrooms had glass doors. The list of oddities runs into the dozens. Could there be a more classic example of the ultimate outcome of "building without a purpose?"

We may think that what we are building is not bizarre like Sarah Winchester's construction project. Let me suggest that unless there is a divine purpose behind why we are doing, God may actually find it as meaningless and bizarre as the Sarah Winchester Mystery House. Paul addresses this very issue in 1 Corinthians 3:12-15 when he says,

> "Now if any man builds on the foundation with gold, silver, precious stones, wood, hay, straw, each man's work will become evident; for the day will show it because it is to be revealed with fire, and the fire itself will test the quality of each man's work. If any man's work which he has built on it remains, he will receive a reward. If any man's work is burned up, he will suffer loss; but he himself will be saved, yet so as through fire."

May I ask, "What foundation are you building on? What materials are you building with? And why are you building what you are building?"

I think John Wesley had it right when he said, "Gain all you can. Save all you can. Give all you can." If we adhere to this compelling "financial triad" as we labor on our building projects, we will be building on a solid foundation utilizing building materials of heavenly "gold, silver, and precious stones." And in our building efforts we will discover that we are indeed living life on purpose.

FOOD FOR THOUGHT

1. How might John Wesley's statement "Gain all you can, save all you can, give all you can" change the way you are currently working, handling money and giving?

2. How is what you are currently doing with your time, your talents and your treasures helping you to fulfill your unique life-purpose?

3. If you continue on the course in which your life is now headed, will you be happy with what you have spent your life "building"?

CHAPTER FIVE

How Do You Calculate How Much You Are Worth?

Often this question is answered with another question, "That depends, who wants to know?" If the Internal Revenue Service is asking, we attempt to make everything appear to be worth as little as possible. We will apply minority and lack of marketability discounts, utilize low appraisals, apply book value, etc. – attempting to minimize our worth. If, on the other hand, it is our banker who is asking, we amazingly become worth considerably more as we attempt to paint the most optimistic, best-case-scenario picture to our lender.

May I suggest, however, that as believers, we need to answer this question in a different way. If we want to most accurately calculate how much we are really worth, we need to utilize three entirely different types of "valuation methods."

Valuation Method #1

We Need to Value Our Life Worth Rather Than Our Net Worth

Many years ago an older, wealthy gentleman shared his story with me. His singular goal in life was to become a millionaire. He imagined this task like climbing a sheer cliff wall. One hand of rock after another, slowly, inch by inch he climbed it. He said, "After spending virtually my entire adult life struggling to get to the top, I was at last able to reach up and grab the top of the cliff. Then slowly I was able to pull myself up to finally, after all these years, see what was there. And do you know what I saw when I pulled myself up," he asked? "Nothing. There was absolutely nothing there." How tragically sad.

The last thing we should want to do is spend our lives climbing the ladder of success only to realize once we finally do reach the top that our ladder is leaning against the wrong wall. And all that we really wanted in life we do not have and all we do have is not what we really want.

Jesus told us, "…a man's life does not consist in the abundance of his possessions" (Luke 12:15, niv). He adds in the parable of the sower, "…the deceitfulness of riches and the desires for other things enter in and choke the word…" (Mark 4:19, nasb). If you are valuing your net worth more than your life worth, you are indeed climbing up the wrong ladder.

So what is your life worth? Paul reminds us, "But God demonstrates His own love toward us, in that while we were yet sinners, Christ died for us" (Romans 5:8, nasb). John adds, "See how great a love the Father has bestowed on us, that we would be called children of God; and such we are" (I John 3:1, nasb). This glorious truth makes us exceedingly valuable.

Some years ago a good friend and client of mine, John Bandimere, invited me to attend his big national drag race event. He gave me a pass that let me go up to his personal tower suite with air conditioned comfort, eat all the free food I wanted, and sit in the best seats at the track. I got to go right down on the track's starting line and he even took me into the pit area. It was an incredible thrill. I felt so important that day. I wanted to tell everyone as I walked around with my VIP pass hanging around my neck, "I personally know the owner of this place!" As I was basking in the thrill of my VIP status, it occurred to me this is exactly the same attitude we ought to have as we travel through life –walking around proudly saying, "I personally know the Owner of this place and that makes me somebody important!"

Our real worth in this life will never be found in the stuff we collect; it will be found in the fact that we personally know the Owner!

Using Valuation Method #1, what are you really worth?

Valuation Method #2

We Need to Value Our Internal Acquisitions Rather Than Our External Acquisitions

Paul addresses just how important it is to be pursuing internal, spiritual acquisitions and not material, external ones. He says, "But those who desire to be rich fall into temptation, into a snare, into many senseless and harmful desires that plunge people into ruin and destruction. For the love of money is a root of all kinds of evils. It is through this craving that some have wandered away from the faith and pierced themselves with many pangs. But as for you, O man of God, flee these things [external acquisitions]. Pursue righteousness, godliness, faith, love, steadfastness, gentleness" [internal acquisitions] (I Timothy 6:9-11, esv).

Paul goes on to specifically encourage women to focus on internal, spiritual acquisitions and not external, material ones when he instructs them, "Your adornment should be not an exterior one, consisting of braided hair or gold jewelry or fine clothing, but the interior disposition of the heart, consisting in the imperishable quality of a gentle and peaceful spirit, so precious in the sight of God" (I Peter 3:3-4, NJB).

35

How diligently are you seeking to internally acquire the mind and nature of Christ? This is what Paul says is "precious [valuable] in the sight of God."

There is no more poignant expression of the folly of valuing what we are worth by our external, material acquisitions instead of by our internal, spiritual ones than when Jesus confronts the Laodiceans in Revelation 3:17. He exposes them saying, "For you say, 'I am rich, I have prospered, and I need nothing' [external acquisitions], not realizing that you are wretched, pitiable, poor, blind, and naked" [internal acquisitions] (esv). The Laodiceans were valuing the wrong balance sheet.

Whenever I read this passage, I cannot help but remember the fairy tale, The Emperor's New Clothes. Two conmen convince the Emperor that the material they are making his new clothes with is so fine that idiots and fools are unable to even see it. The Emperor, in order to avoid being labeled an idiot or a fool, convinces himself that he can see the new clothes and proudly parades down the streets of the city in his underwear believing that he was clothed in the finest garments, when in reality he was clothed in nothing at all. The very thing he was trying to avoid is the very thing he ended up proving – he, like the Laodiceans, was indeed a fool and an idiot.

This is what will happen to us, if we choose to calculate what we are worth based upon our external acquisitions instead of our internal ones. We must understand this, "What the world esteems greatly [external acquisitions], God disregards and what God esteems greatly [internal acquisitions], the world disregards."

Using Valuation Method #2, what are you really worth?

Valuation Method #3

We Need to Value Our Eternal Assets Rather Than Our Temporal Assets

The Bible is very clear that our temporal assets will do us no good after we leave this planet. Solomon tells us (and he ought to know), "Wealth is worthless in the day of wrath [temporal assets], but righteousness [eternal assets] delivers from death" (Proverbs 11:4, niv).

Jesus reminds us that even a temporal balance sheet that would include everything on earth is still wholly worthless on the judgment day. He tells us, "For what does it profit a man to gain the whole world [temporal assets], and forfeit his soul [eternal assets]?" (Mark 8:36, nasb)

You may recall in Daniel where God writes on the wall an unreadable message to King Belshazzar. He calls for Daniel to interpret God's message. Daniel translates, "You praised the gods of silver and gold, of bronze, iron, wood and stone… [temporal assets]. But you did not honor the God who holds in his hand your life and all your ways…You have been weighed on the scales and found wanting [eternal assets]" (Daniel 5:23b, 27, niv). We must be ever mindful that on God's eternal scales, our accumulated, temporal assets, no matter how great they might be, weigh nothing.

Because of this, Jesus commands us, "Do not lay up for yourselves treasures upon earth… [temporal assets], but lay up for yourselves treasures in heaven…" [eternal assets] (Matthew 6:19-20, nasb).

Receiving rewards (treasures) in heaven is not taught in most churches. But the Bible is very clear that even though our salvation cannot be earned by any good works, our "rewards in heaven" will be directly tied to our good works. Twenty-nine times the Greek word for rewards is used in the New Testament. Here are some of the ways the New Testament tells us to grow our eternal assets (rewards/treasures) in heaven: accepting persecution (Matthew 5:10-12), loving our enemies (Luke 6:35), giving generously (Matthew 6:2-4), praying (Matthew 6:6), fasting (Matthew 6:18), showing hospitality (Matthew 10:41), showing kindness towards others (Mark 9:41), doing good deeds (I Corinthians 3:10, Colossians 3:24), and sharing our faith (I Corinthians 3:8, I Corinthians 9:17-18).

When we calculate what we are worth, are we looking at what we have here and now or what we will have then and there? What we keep now, we will lose forever and what we lose now, we will keep forever.

How much would you be worth if you were to eternally relocate today? This question ought to give all of us cause to pause and reflect.

Using Valuation Method #3, what are you really worth?

If we want to know how much we are really worth, we cannot use the world's valuation methods because they are inaccurate and misleading and will only provide us with a distorted sense of worth. God's valuation methods, on the other hand, are true and accurate and by utilizing them as our standard measure of worth, we can be sure that in God's economy, we can be indeed rich in both this life and the next, regardless of what our current balance sheet may show.

FOOD FOR THOUGHT

1. Have you ever considered the idea of making it to the end of your life only to realize that what you really want in life, you do not have and what you do have, you do not really want? How can you keep from ending up at this point?

2. List what the internal assets are that you possess and then answer why you think these should be of greater value to you than the external material assets in your life.

3. Based upon these three new valuation methods to determine your worth, how do they change your perspective on how well off you are?

CHAPTER SIX

Do You Love the World?

The Bible is full of caution lights warning us when we are about to head off course and into spiritual trouble. John issues one of those warnings to us, "Do not love the world or anything in the world. If anyone loves the world, the love of the Father is not in him" (1 John 2:15).

It is quite interesting that John tells us to not love (agape) the world (cosmos) with the very same Greek words that Jesus used when He told us that "God so loved (agape) the world (cosmos)…" (John 3:16). So, since we know that God cannot contradict Himself, there must be a way in which we are to love the world and a way in which we are to not love the world. We can understand this apparent contradiction in the following way.

A spiritually healthy love for the world desires to give something to it [the gospel]. The rest of John 3:16 says, "For God so loved the world that he gave."

A spiritually sick love for the world desires to get something from it I John 2:16 says, "For everything in the world—the cravings of sinful man, the lust of his eyes and the boasting of what he has and does—comes not from the Father but from the world."

What is troubling about John's warning is that it doesn't give us much guidance on how to identify whether we do in fact love the world and the things of the world. Is it enough that we say we love God and we don't love the world or the things of the world? Is our profession enough? I don't know about you, but my words have often betrayed me. I have found on occasion that I am not really what I say I am. (What is on the outside is not what is on the inside.) So, it is necessary for us to look deeper than just our words. We must look at our hearts and observe our actions to determine if we are indeed in love with the world and the things of the world.

I have identified four, flashing, "caution lights" that should warn us that we might indeed have gotten into an illicit love affair with the world and the things of this world.

Caution Light #1

We are falling in love with the world...when we are never quite satisfied with what we have.

Solomon says in Ecclesiastes 5:10, "Whoever loves money never has money enough; whoever loves wealth is never satisfied with his income." Are you truly satisfied with what you have right now? If you never got anything more for the rest of your life would that be ok with you?

Or, do you find yourself drawn to the newest technology gadget, a bigger or better car, another exotic travel destination, the latest fashion, a newer or bigger home, or another way to make more money. Is your life characterized by wanting and getting more stuff?

Solomon again warns us in Ecclesiastes 6:7, "All man's efforts are for his mouth, yet his appetite is never satisfied." Is your appetite satisfied with what you have right now or will it take more?

If "more" is descriptive of the way you think about the things of the world and the way you live in the world, Caution Light #1 is flashing and you may indeed be involved in an illicit love affair with the world that can destroy your pure and holy relationship to your bride groom, Jesus.

Caution Light #2

We are falling in love with the world…when the things we own end up owning us.

Jesus reminded us that we only have one throne and He wants to be on it. He tells us in Matthew 6:24, "No one can serve two masters; for either he will hate the one and love the other, or he will be devoted to one and despise the other. You cannot serve God and wealth."

Demas was one of Paul's mission entourage. Paul is grieved to report to Timothy (II Timothy 4:10) that "Demas, having loved this present world, has deserted me…" That is what happens when we love the world and the things of the world. You cannot have both on the same throne. Jesus tells us in Luke 12:15, "…Beware, and be on your guard against every form of greed; for not even when one has an abundance does his life consist of his possessions." We can own things, but things better not own us.

It is easy enough to get so emotionally attached to our things that we do not want to part with them or give them away. The greater our love for our things, the more tightly we grip them. The great holocaust survivor Corrie Ten Boom often spoke these words of wisdom, "Hold loosely to the things of this life, so that if God requires them of you, it will be easy to let them go."

What was the rich, young ruler's obstacle to following Jesus? "But when the young man heard this statement, he went away grieving; for he was one who owned much property (Matthew 19:22)." He didn't own his possessions. His possessions owned him. And they would not let go of him.

If your find that your things own and control you, Caution Light #2 is flashing and you may indeed be involved in an illicit love affair with the world that can destroy your pure and holy relationship to your bride groom, Jesus.

Caution Light #3

We are falling in love with the world…when worry about losing our things is disrupting our inner peace.

Recent times have certainly given us all ample opportunity to discern if worry about material loss has been disrupting our inner peace. When times are good, we may never even notice Caution Light #3, but when retirement funds plummet, the values of our real estate is in a free fall and our business revenues are off substantially, all this can reveal a love for the world and the things of the world that we may have never really noticed.

Paul reminds us that our financial condition should have nothing to do with our inner peace and contentment in life. He says in Philippians 4:11-12, "Not that I speak from want, for I have learned to be content in whatever circumstances I am. I know how to get along with humble means, and I also know how to live in prosperity; in any and every circumstance I have learned the secret of being filled and going hungry, both of having abundance and suffering need."

Being content when you have a lot is quite easy, but being content with less or much less than we have grown comfortable with can be very unsettling and reveal the actual depth of our affection for the things of this world.

If you have placed your faith in your things instead of the One who has provided those things, you are in danger. Hebrews 13:5 points this out clearly, "Make sure that your character is free from the love of money, being content with what you have; for He Himself has said, 'I will never desert you, nor will I ever forsake you.'"

If we were stripped of all our worldly possessions and stood penniless, would we still be content and filled with inner peace, confident that our loving Father is still on the throne and will never, ever forsake us?

If you are struggling with a disquieted spirit as you worry over your "net worth" falling and your cash flow shrinking, Caution Light #3 is flashing and you may indeed be involved in an illicit love affair with the world that can destroy your pure and holy relationship to your bride groom, Jesus.

Caution Light #4

We are falling in love with the world…when our longing to be there is diminished by our affection for what we have here.

Mrs. Jones asked her eight year old Sunday school class, "How many of you would like to go to Heaven?" Every child in the class raised his hand except Billy. Mrs. Jones asked curiously, "Billy, don't you want to go to Heaven?" He replied, "Sure I do, I just thought you were taking up a bus load right now!" Billy was glad to go to Heaven, just not right now.

When I was a teenager my grandmother had a heart attack and fell into unconsciousness. Her four daughters (one was my mother) got together and made the decision for the doctors to insert a pacemaker to keep her alive. I remember to this day how furious my grandmother was when she awoke in the hospital and realized that she was still here. She so longed to go to be with the Lord that the life saving intervention of a pacemaker only prevented her from getting where she longed to go. My grandmother's unhappy reaction to still being here is etched permanently in my mind.

I am reminded of what Paul said in II Corinthians 5:8, "prefer rather to be absent from the body and to be at home with the Lord." If you were given the choice today, would you prefer to go be with the Lord or would you prefer to stay here? Are you more like Billy or my grandmother?

If you have nothing more than a casual interest in being there, Caution Light #4 is flashing and you may indeed be involved in an illicit love affair with the world that can destroy your pure and holy relationship to your bride groom, Jesus.

The alluring appeal of the world and the things of the world are very subtle and can sneak up on any of us at any time and begin wrapping its insidious tentacles around us and before we even realize we are trapped, we are overcome. This is the very thing the parable of the seeds describes in Matthew 13:22, "And the one on whom seed was sown among the thorns, this is the man who hears the word, and the worry of the world and the deceitfulness of wealth choke the word, and it becomes unfruitful."

As we continue to live in this materialistic culture of ours, may we all keep our eyes carefully peeled for these four caution lights so we might not unintentionally end up becoming an illicit lover of the world and the things of the world. Hebrews 12:1b-2a challenges us, "Let us also lay aside every encumbrance and the sin which so easily entangles us, and let us run with endurance the race that is set before us, fixing our eyes on Jesus, the author and perfecter of (our) faith...." May this be so for all of us.

FOOD FOR THOUGHT

1. Corrie Ten Boom tells us to hold loosely to the things of this life, so that if God requires them of you, it will be easy to let go of them. Consider how this thought could change how you view your personal life and possessions?

2. How does your "contentment" line up to Paul's in Philippians 4:11-12? What areas do you struggle to fully find contentment and why?

3. When you find yourself fearful about the loss of material things or a reduced current lifestyle, how do you react? How does that reaction reflect your relationship with the Father?

CHAPTER SEVEN

Living on Less

Recently I received an email with the subject line, "You can live on less when you have more to live for." This statement so struck me that I literally stopped my expeditious handling of all my emails and just pondered this profound and thought-provoking statement. "You can live on less when you have more to live for."

This is not a statement describing an involuntary "belt-tightening" when economic circumstances force one to reduce a preferred lifestyle. It is talking about someone who chooses to voluntarily reduce his/her current lifestyle – a willing reduction.

Routinely, one of the primary objectives in planning for those who have surplus cash flow and excess wealth is to ensure that they are able to maintain their current lifestyle while doing all their inheritance and charitable planning. The key word here is "maintain." In other words, "I am willing to be as charitable as possible with my "wealth" as long as it does not negatively impact my current lifestyle.

But this statement suggests that there might actually be some reasons why a person would want to reduce his rate of personal consumption (what we call the "burn rate") to intentionally "live on less."

So what might happen that would lead a person who could live on more –

much more – to happily and willingly choose to live on less? This quote tells us. They have found something "more to live for" – something that is more valuable and more fulfilling to them than self-consumption.

As I pondered this statement, I asked myself, "What would it take for me or anyone else to willingly choose to live on less?" I concluded that in order to choose to live on less there would have to be a change in one or more of these three areas – (1.) one's Perspective, (2.) one's Priorities, and/or (3.) one's Purpose.

A Change in Perspective

I travel a lot and in order to avoid feeling "claustrophobic" on the plane, I always try to get an aisle seat, but on occasion, I find myself "trapped" in a window seat. If there is any redemption to a window seat it is the view. I must confess that there is nothing that gives me a more realistic perspective of life than looking at the world from 35,000 feet.

Elevation does seem to give us a substantially different perspective on the "things of earth." If we could pile up all of Bill Gate's and Warren Buffet's "stuff" in one place, it might not even be noticeable from the viewpoint of 35,000 feet. How much more insignificant are things if viewed from the footstool of Heaven. If a man were to see the trappings of his current lifestyle from the perspective of Heaven, he might just conclude there is undoubtedly something "more to live for" than the insignificant and temporary creature comforts of his current lifestyle.

Matthew 13:44-46 gives us a picture of what happens when someone's perspective changes. Jesus said, "The kingdom of heaven is like treasure hidden in a field. When a man found it, he hid it again, and then in his joy went and sold all he had and bought that field. Again, the kingdom of heaven is like a merchant looking for fine pearls. When he found one of great value, he went away and sold everything he had and bought it."

Their perception of the value of their current possessions was totally redefined when they discovered something they perceived to be of far greater worth. There is an old riddle, "Do you know how to get a bone out of a dog's mouth?" The answer is, "Offer him a bone with more meat on it."

We will gladly "live on less" when our perspective is reoriented and reveals something "more to live for." By downsizing, we would actually be upgrading!

A Change in Priorities

We all have a list of priorities. They are seldom put in writing and placed on the refrigerator, but we all have them stored away somewhere in the recesses of our consciousness. When given a choice between two options, our list of priorities kicks in and we choose the one highest on the list. This is true with our time and our treasures.

If your child has a ball game and you also have an opportunity to go play golf with your best friends, which you choose will demonstrate your priorities. If you had to choose between helping your child with their college expenses or buying a new car, your pre-set priorities will determine which choice you make. And, likewise, when given the choice between deploying your material resources for Kingdom purposes or buying a bigger home or the latest luxury car, your priorities will determine your choice.

We recently were hired by a younger couple who had done extremely well professionally and financially. The husband and wife came from nothing and as their businesses grew and their income skyrocketed, so did their lifestyle. They found themselves with an extravagant home, the newest and most expensive vehicles, and all the toys and trappings of a family who had "made it."

But something happened to this couple along the way. God began to burden them with the call of the great commission and the need to get the gospel out while there was still time – before Jesus' return. And quite apart from any influence by me, the husband had already made the decision that he wanted to become one of the greatest Christian philanthropists in history. In order to do this, they have already begun to cut their lifestyle consumption by multiples in order to have more available to deploy for Kingdom work. They are selling their "mansion" and moving into a modest home. They are buying cheaper used cars and intend to drive them until they cannot be driven anymore. His goal now is to build as many businesses as he can and grow them as much as he can so he can give as much as possible to the Kingdom during the rest of his life. Talk about a change in priorities!

For a man to choose to "live on less" it will require a radical reordering of existing priorities and these newly reordered priorities likely will reveal to him that there is much "more to live for."

A Change in Purpose

In one of my slideshow presentations I ask the question, "What on earth am I doing with all this wealth?" I think it is an imminently practical and important question that each of us needs to answer. And how we answer that question will be reflected by what we choose to do with our material possessions. Did God give us excess material possessions to increase our lifestyle or to increase our Kingdom impact? Did our Father provide us with surplus resources so we could be "rich in lifestyle" or so we could be "rich in good deeds" (I Timothy 6:18)?

I can think of no more powerful example of this statement, "You can live on less when you have more to live for," than what is vividly demonstrated in the life and death of Jesus himself. II Corinthians 8:9 tells us, "For you know the grace of our Lord Jesus Christ, that though He was rich, yet for your sake He became poor, that you through His poverty might become rich."

Jesus was the richest "man" in the universe and yet facing a divine purpose that collided with His exalted place in Heaven, He willingly "humbled Himself" and "made Himself nothing" (Philippians 2:6-8) and came to a dirty, sin-filled, remote planet to accomplish this divine purpose. He downsized from a throne in Heaven to a cross on Calvary.

Jesus was pursuing a purpose that required Him to radically reduce His preferred lifestyle in order to carry out a grand and noble purpose – the redemption of the entire human race.

I think none of us can escape the probing question that if Jesus, being rich, became poor for us so that we could be rich, what does He intend for us to do with those riches we have gained from His voluntary poverty? We need to soberly ponder this question.

For a man to choose to "live on less" it will require a radical reorientation of his life purpose that will reveal to him that there is indeed a greater life purpose that will give him even "more to live for."

"You can live on less when you have more to live for." Maybe each of us ought to humbly reconsider our current perspective, our current priorities, and our current purpose. It may be that if we honestly assess these three areas of our lives and humbly attempt to align them with the perspective, priorities, and purpose of Christ, we might just find to our surprise that we will be glad to "live on less" because in so doing we have found "more to live for" – much more.

FOOD FOR THOUGHT

1. Have you ever considered that Jesus willingly downsized from a throne in Heaven to a cross on Calvary? How does that truth change how you view your material possessions?

2. If Jesus, being rich, became poor for you so that you could be rich, what does He intend for you to do with those riches that you have gained from His voluntary poverty?

3. For you personally, what would the "more to live for" have to be for you to gladly choose to "live on less"?

CHAPTER EIGHT

What is Your Most Valuable Possession?

What is your most valuable possession? When you first read this question your mind may quickly scroll through the list of all your possessions, looking for your asset with the highest value. For most people, you hear their home is their most valuable asset. For those whose net worth is larger, that is seldom the case. Instead, is it might be their business, one of their real estate holdings, or their investment portfolio? No matter which asset you may select as the most valuable, you will have picked the wrong one. Our materialistic culture drives us to think of our things when we think of our valuables, but there are other non-material things that are worth much more.

I would suggest to you that the correct answer to this question can be found by looking on a different balance sheet. Many years ago I heard Bob Buford, a self-made multimillionaire and author of the book Halftime: Changing your Game Plan from Success to Significance, speak at a conference. Right in the middle of the presentation he made a comment that was so profound and struck me so deeply that I do not think I really heard anything else he said for the rest of his presentation. He paused, gave a reflective look, and then commented, "It seems insane to me that a person would be willing to trade what he has a shortage of—time—in order to gain more of what he already has a surplus of—wealth." You cannot read this once and fully absorb it, so look at it again. "It seems insane to me that a person would be willing to trade what he has a shortage of—time—in order to gain more of what he already has a surplus of—wealth."

So, what is your most valuable asset? It is the time that you still have "banked" in this life. Your "time on this earth" account is all too quickly shrinking with every day that passes. And the most troubling part of this time account is that we cannot see how much we have left. Is it days, months, years, decades?

We often hear people ask the question, "How do you spend your time...?" This is a very accurate way to phrase how we use our time: we spend it. Unlike your financial accounts that you can make additional deposits into and build the account in the future, you can make no additional deposits into your time account. The total number of days allotted to us was deposited into our time account before we were even conceived. King David confirms this in Psalm 139:16, when he acknowledges, "And in Your book were written all the days that were ordained for me, when as yet there was not one of them." So, all of us will spend our time on something—and once it is spent, it is gone.

The truth of Bob Buford's comment is nowhere more clearly illustrated than in the story of the rich farmer we looked at earlier. After another excessive bumper crop season, he says,

> This is what I will do: I will tear down my barns and build larger ones, and there I will store all my grain and my goods. And I will say to my soul, 'Soul, you have many goods laid up for many years to come; take your ease, eat, drink and be merry.' But God said to him, 'You fool! This very night your soul is required of you; and now who will own what you have prepared?'
> Luke 12:18-20

How pathetically sad. He was willing to trade what he had almost nothing left of—time—in order to gain more of what he already had a surplus of—wealth. And then to add insult to his folly, God goes on to say of this man, "So is the man who stores up treasure for himself, and is not rich toward God" (Luke 12:21). He did not die rich—he died broke.

In Psalm 90:12, Moses asks God to help him use his time account wisely. He prays, "So teach us to number our days, that we may present to You a heart of wisdom." Paul said it this way in Ephesians 5:15-16, "Therefore be careful how you walk, not as unwise men but as wise, making the most of your time, because the days are evil." And not only are the days "evil," they are also very limited.

It seems to me that we need to manage our time account with even greater care than we manage our investment accounts. And we should be very leery about making any withdrawals out of our limited time account— "spending our time"—in order to make additional deposits into our temporal, investment accounts or even worse wasting our time on things that really don't matter.

I have consistently heard from many Christian families their honest acknowledgment that they have more money to give than they have time. It is considerably easier for these believers to make a gift from their material possessions than it is to make a gift from their over-used and ever shrinking time account.

Keep this in mind: it is not in how much of our stuff we give; it is in how much of ourselves we give that allows us to fully experience the joy and blessing of giving. As a nation, we have far too much material prosperity to experience much real sacrificial giving, regardless of how much or how little of it we personally possess. But we all have precious little to give from our time account, but this is where we, who are rich by the world's standard, learn to give like those who have little – by any standard.
More and more families are catching the vision and seeing the power of short-term, family mission trips to needy countries. Can you guess what

proves to be the greatest obstacle in pulling off such a trip? It is not typically the cost. That is frankly the easiest part of the trip. The hardest part of the trip is finding the time for all of the members of the family to make such a trip—to make a difference. The problem is the time, not the money.

When I was a young boy, I spent a good bit of time visiting my grandmother. She was a zealous and committed Christian woman and everywhere you turned in her small home, there were signs of her faith—a Bible on the coffee table—plaques and pictures on the walls—Bible verses on the refrigerator. There was one plaque in particular that made a significant impact on my thinking as a young boy. I did not realize it then, but I do now. The little plaque read, "Only one life 'twill soon be past, only what's done for Christ will last." Because of that compelling thought, my entire life, for the most part, has been one continuous attempt to use the brief time that God has allotted me to do something that will matter for eternity. Without this ultimate, eternal objective as our singular focus, life is correctly summed up by Solomon, "All of it is meaningless, a chasing after the wind" (Ecclesiastes 2:17 niv).

What is your most valuable asset? How are you using your most valuable asset to do something that will last for eternity? Our cry should be, to paraphrase Isaiah 6:8, "Here I am Lord, [spend] me."

FOOD FOR THOUGHT

1. Do you receive more joy from writing a check (giving money) or getting personally involved (giving of yourself/your time)? What are you doing to be more engaged in both ways?

2. The plaque mentioned read, "Only one life 'twill soon be past. Only what's done for Christ will last." What could you do with your limited remaining time on earth to accomplish something with your life that will last for eternity?

3. If you were to learn that you only had 30 days left on this earth, how would the use of your remaining days change? What does that tell you about your life priorities?

CHAPTER NINE

Housekeeping Matters

Many of you have likely attended a conference where someone gets up at the beginning of the conference to go over important housekeeping matters you need to know. Housekeeping matters are often important minor details that will help the conference run more smoothly – like hotel checkout time, restroom locations, scheduled break times, airport shuttle departures and so on.

However, I would like to suggest an alternate understanding of the phrase, that being "it matters how we keep our house" – in other words housekeeping really matters. The house I am suggesting that we need to be keeping is not the one made of wood and bricks that contains our stuff, but is the one made of flesh and blood that houses us and the Holy Spirit.

Paul tells us in I Corinthians 3:16, "Do you not know that you are God's temple and that God's Spirit dwells in you?" Notice our body is God's temple and as such we need to treat it as our mutual dwelling place.

There are three important reasons why it really does matter how well we are keeping our house.

First: *Housekeeping Matters* <u>*Because it is Commanded*</u>

I often hear people make off-handed comments suggesting that God isn't all that concerned about what we eat or how well we take care of our bodies – because, after all, we are going to get a new, perfect one later.

They will often quote Romans 14:14 where Paul assesses food in general, "I know and am persuaded in the Lord Jesus that nothing is unclean in itself..." They conclude that anything that can be chewed up and swallowed is acceptable fare for consumption and God really doesn't care what we consume.

Regarding exercise I hear frequently mentioned I Timothy 4:8 where Paul says, "for bodily discipline is only of little profit, but godliness is profitable for all things..." They conclude that because spiritual exercise is of greater value than physical exercise, physical exercise is unimportant.

But as caretakers of bodies that do not belong to us, I would like to suggest that we consider a broader perspective on the feeding and exercise of the bodies that God has entrusted to us.

Most believers are quite familiar with I Peter 1:15-16 which says, "but as He who called you is holy, you also be holy in all your conduct, since it is written, 'You shall be holy, for I am holy.'" Few realize that this is actually a quote from the Old Testament. And it may surprise you to know the context of where this phrase "be holy for I am holy" comes from.

In Leviticus 11:44-45 God is giving dietary directions to the children of Israel, "For I am the Lord your God. Consecrate yourselves therefore, and be holy, for I am holy. You shall not defile yourselves with any swarming thing that crawls on the ground. For I am the Lord who brought you up out of the land of Egypt to be your God. You shall therefore be holy, for I am holy."

This concept of being holy for I am holy comes right out of the middle of a chapter where God is telling His children what to eat and what not to eat. Keep in mind the word "holy" also means "pure." Apparently God does not want his children to defile the houses He has given them by consuming things that will physically defile (pollute/abuse) those physical houses.

We must understand that how we feed our house is not a means to spiritual approval. Paul points this out in I Corinthians 8:8, "Food will not commend us to God. We are no worse off (spiritually) if we do not eat, and no better off (spiritually) if we do." How we keep our house will have no affect on us after we leave this life. However, it can and will have a massive and often long-term affect on us while we are still in this life.

In spite of his comment, Paul still understood the need for strict physical discipline and the tragic, spiritual ramifications for failing to maintain such discipline. In I Corinthians 9:27 he says, "but I discipline my body and make it my slave, so that, after I have preached to others, I myself will not be disqualified."

What we eat and drink and how much we eat and drink has continually been an important physical issue with considerable spiritual ramifications for many centuries. It was as far back as the 4th century when the church first listed gluttony as one of the seven deadly/cardinal sins.

Physical housekeeping really does matter.

Second: Housekeeping Matters *Because it is Worship*

Paul gives us a second perspective on the extent that housekeeping matters when he challenges us in Romans 12:1, "Therefore I urge you, brethren, by the mercies of God, to present your bodies a living and holy sacrifice, acceptable to God, which is your spiritual service of worship."

Paul makes this same point in answering his own rhetorical question in I Corinthians 6:19-20, "Do you not know that your body is a temple of the Holy Spirit who is in you, whom you have from God, and that you are not your own? For you have been bought with a price: therefore glorify God in your body." We are to be glorifying God with and in our bodies.

In both these passages Paul connects our physical and spiritual lives together. He tells us that how well we keep our house should glorify Him and be an outward, physical expression of our worship of Him.

Is how you keep your body an act of worship for you? Does the current condition of your house bring Him glory? Is your housekeeping a clear demonstration of your loving and careful management of the dwelling place He has entrusted to you?

Physical housekeeping really does matter.

Third: Housekeeping Matters *Because it is Smart*

Even if God hadn't commanded us to take good care of our houses and even if He hadn't told us that we worship Him by what we do with our bodies, there is still a third entirely pragmatic reason to take good care of our bodies that should itself be a compelling enough reason to be responsible housekeepers.

It has been my observation over the years that any asset left unmanaged becomes a liability. I have found no exception to this maxim whether it be materials things, relationships or businesses. You name it. If you buy a new car and never service the car, your asset will eventually turn into a liability. Likewise, if you do not properly "service" your body, it will eventually become a liability too – sooner than it should.

The Center for Disease Control's report on the health of Americans is staggering. It estimates that of the 300 million Americans, 63% are considered overweight or obese; 80% of Americans over 25 are overweight; 78% of American's are not even meeting basic activity level recommendations.

According to former U.S. Surgeon General, Dr. C. Everett Koop of the 2.4 million deaths that occur in the United States each year, 75% are the result of avoidable nutritional factor diseases. In other words, 75% of Americans are suffering and ultimately dying prematurely from self-inflicted degenerative diseases due to the poor care and feeding of their houses.

Can you imagine the hundreds of millions of dollars of God's money God's people are needlessly spending on drugs, surgeries and healthcare to attempt to recover from the physical maladies that they have brought upon themselves by failing to make good long term lifestyle decisions? God's asset has been turned into a liability.

It is just smart to do whatever we possibly can to allow our houses to retain their vigor, their health and their vitality as long as possible. Because of the curse of Adam, all of our bodies are going to eventually wear out and cease to operate. But doesn't it make sense to postpone that time as long as possible by taking good care of our houses so they remain an asset that God can use for His purposes and His glory? The more healthy we remain, the more useful we can be for God's Kingdom and for His purposes.

If you knew that the next car you bought was going to be the last car you would ever own; if you knew that it was going to have to last for decades and even though there are some replacement parts available, you were going to have to live with whatever condition it was in, would you care for your car differently? I would. How much more should we treat our most valuable physical asset with meticulous care? This is the only body we are going to get this side of glory.

If you would like to develop a healthier lifestyle – become a better housekeeper, I would suggest you start with the book, The Maker's Diet by Jordon Rubin and then go from there. And don't forget the Owner's Manual. You would be absolutely amazed at what God has told us in His Manual about health, disease, diet, exercise, etc.

I hope as you pray and seek the mind of the Lord on this important but often ignored area of stewardship that you will come to agree with me that housekeeping matters.

FOOD FOR THOUGHT

1. Consider how being in good shape physically actually helps you to be in better shape spiritually and emotionally. What do you need to do to get in better shape for the Lord?

2. Why do you think we often take better care of our cars than we do our bodies that God entrusted to us to live in?

3. With all this new information on good housekeeping and its importance, what changes do you intend to make to do a better job of caring for His temple?

CHAPTER TEN

Giving Generously or Living Generously?

For many years I have been actively promoting the idea of generous giving. I have written books and articles about it; I have taught on it; and I have helped affluent families do it. To say the least, generosity is for me both a calling and a passion. But quite recently, the Lord has shown me through a sequence of unrelated events that I still have a lot to learn about what it means to be generous. Let me tell you the stories.

Recently on Sunday morning, at the end of our worship time, the worship minister announced that we were about to watch an extraordinary video about a couple in our church. As the video rolls, I am surprised – I know the husband, B.J. because I have played basketball with him at church for the past few years. I liked him from the very first time we played ball together. B.J. is a young man in his late 20s, has a successful money management practice and is an extremely talented athlete. Since I knew one of the main characters in this video, I proudly nudged my wife and said, "I know him!"

My excitement turned to embarrassment as he and his wife shared their story. B.J.'s wife had a high school friend who was very ill and in need of a kidney transplant. Both of them immediately said to themselves, "Maybe we could give her one of our kidneys." Well, it seemed reasonable to me that B.J.'s wife might want to give her good friend one of her kidneys, but as it turned out B.J.'s kidney was the perfect match. So without hesitation he donated one of his kidneys to his wife's high school friend. They shared that it just seemed like the right thing to do. B.J. had an extra kidney and this girl had none.

I was stunned. I wouldn't give one of my kidneys to one of my wife's friends. I would not even consider it. Of course I would give one to my wife or one of my children if they needed it, but to one of my wife's friends? Don't get me wrong, I am all about giving of my time, talent and treasure, but giving my torso – my body parts? That was a level of giving that entirely surpassed my current concept of generosity.

Just a few days later, I was ready to board a plane to return home from a business trip. I was first in line and was looking forward to getting comfortable in my first class seat and then "zoning out" on the flight home. (I often get upgraded for free.)

Just prior to our boarding, a very heavy, crippled man had been escorted down the jetway in his wheelchair to board the plane. So I waited patiently for the call for first class to board. However, just as they began to announce the first class boarding, another guy cuts right in front of me and hands the attendant his boarding pass. His rude manner and obviously arrogant attitude irritated me.

As we got to the bottom of the jetway, four airline staff were having difficulty getting the heavy, crippled man out of his wheelchair and into the airline wheelchair needed to get him on the plane. This delay was causing a back up in the jetway. No one was able to board because they were right in front of the plane door. So here I am standing and stewing over this rude guy who cut in front of me while I was waiting to get on the plane. I stood there a little impatiently watching the airline employees working futilely to get this crippled man into the airline wheelchair.

Then, the bomb fell. The guy who cut in front of me calls out to the flight crew, "Hey, let me help you." So he drops his bags and hurries over to them and helps get the man into the plane wheelchair. I was so ashamed. I was standing there just like the line-cutter was, but the thought never even crossed my mind to offer any help. Of all the people standing there watching this happen, this guy who I was convinced was so selfish and full of himself was the one who volunteered to help.

Unfortunately, the humiliation wasn't over. When they finally get the man in the wheelchair and through the plane door, Mr. Helpful then says to the airline staff. "Let me go back and get his bag for you." He comes back off the plane, grabs the man's bag, which by the way, is right at my feet and takes it back into the plane to him. Yet, another missed opportunity for me to live generously.

By this point I am feeling very convicted about my lack of generosity. Interestingly enough, it turns out the line-cutter is sitting right across the aisle from me in first class. I told him I appreciated his willingness to help the crippled man. He smiled and said, "It wasn't anything." To him, it wasn't anything, but to me it proved that of the two of us, I was the one who was selfish and full of myself, not him.

But God still wasn't finished rocking my generosity world. As I am finally relaxing in my first class aisle seat, the passengers in economy start filing past me. I hear a woman immediately behind me ask this soldier who is standing right next to me, "Soldier, what seat are you in?" He says, "21B." "One of the dreaded middle seats in the back," I thought. She then says to him, "Would you like to sit here?" The soldier hesitated, but the woman insisted that he take her first class seat and she would go back and sit in his middle economy seat.

Humbled again! This is all happening right next to me. Know that I deeply appreciate what our military does for us as a country and for me as one of its citizens. I have even thanked soldiers for their service on many occasions. But the thought of offering this soldier my first class seat and taking a middle seat in economy class on a packed plane was another indicator of just how limited my generosity really is.

I have been mulling these experiences over in my mind for a few weeks and I wanted to share with you the main lesson that I think God has taught me through this. The lesson is this: I can be generous in how I give without being generous in how I live. Conversely, I have also learned that a person who lives generously always gives generously.

In other words, we may be willing to be extremely generous in giving what we want to give where we want to give it. But with what we don't want to give we can actually find ourselves being just as selfish and tight-fisted as the infamous Ebenezer Scrooge. Living generously, not giving generously needs to be our goal.

I have identified three characteristics of people who model generous living:

Characteristic #1
Generous Living is Open-Hearted

Those who live generously are open-hearted and alert to find people who are struggling, hurting or in pain. They empathize with those whose world is difficult and they enjoy trying to make it better.

Characteristic #2
Generous Living is Open-Minded

The minds of those who live generously are always thinking about creative ways to bless and encourage others in both great and small ways. They are consciously engaged in their world and the lives of those around them, poised to show generosity to anyone whenever the opportunity presents itself.

Characteristic #3
Generous Living is Open-Handed

The resources of those who live generously, all of them – (time, talent, treasure [and torso]), are ready to be gladly given whenever a need or an opportunity is discovered. When it is within their power to respond, they relish the privilege to make a difference and bless the life of another – friend or stranger. They live out the extreme attitude, "What is mine is yours and you can have it."

In these three recent experiences it has been vividly demonstrated to me that the key to living a generous life is easy to understand. It is, however, excruciatingly difficult to live because of what it requires of us – a radical change in our self-assessment. Paul tells us in Philippians 2:3, "…but with humility of mind let each of you regard one another as more important than himself." There it is – in just one part of one verse – "regard one another as more important than himself."

If we can wholly embrace this radical change in our self-assessment – and truly come to believe that others are more important than ourselves, we will be completely transformed into not just people who are giving generously, but more importantly into people who are living generously – who reflect an open-hearted, open-minded and open-handed life. If we really want to achieve maximum Kingdom impact in our lives, may I suggest that we expand our focus to not just giving generously, but more importantly to living generously.

FOOD FOR THOUGHT

1. Which of the three stories shared were you able to most relate to and why?

2. Think of a time in which you have given generously without having lived generously. What are you going to do to more fully embrace a generous lifestyle?

3. Think of a time in which you walked right past an opportunity to be "generous in how you live"? How can you alter your awareness of these opportunities so that, starting today, they will no longer pass you by?

CHAPTER ELEVEN

Are You Living Like a Bucket or a Pipe?

Are you living like a "bucket" or a "pipe"? This is a rather odd metaphorical question, is it not? Yet, it is only odd until you consider the purpose of a bucket and the purpose of a pipe. A bucket is designed to hold things (liquids, dirt, etc.). A pipe is designed to convey things through it (fluids, gases, etc.). The bucket holds what it receives and the pipe transfers on what it receives. So, in regards to the wealth that God has graciously entrusted to you, let me ask, "Are you living your life like a bucket or a pipe?" Are you holding on or passing on?

The Way of the Bucket

It is easy enough to live like a bucket and there are three reasons why we can indeed find ourselves living like a bucket.

#1: We can find ourselves living like a bucket when we ignore the ultimate end of all buckets.

I saw a bumper sticker some time ago that read, "He who dies with the most toys wins." I thought, "What an accurate way to express the world's view of life and possessions." But it immediately occurred to me that yes, this is true if the game of life is all about accumulation, but the sad tragedy is that he who dies with the most toys still dies and then someone else will get to play with all his toys.

David reminds us in Psalm 49:16-17 niv,

Do not be overawed when a man grows rich (when he has a big bucket and it is full), when the splendor of his house increases; for he will take nothing with him when he dies, his splendor will not descend with him.

God condemns the rich farmer we discussed previously for this very thing: "God said to him, 'You fool! This very night your soul is required of you; and now who will own what you have prepared (what is left in your bucket)? So is the man who stores up treasure for himself (kept his own bucket full), and is not rich toward God" (Luke 12:20-21).

What we keep in our bucket will eventually leak out, be stolen, taxed, evaporate, or spilled out when you "kick the bucket." This should give us reason to pause as we consider the folly of living life like a bucket.

#2: We can find ourselves living like a bucket when we bestow on ourselves "Most Important Person" status.

When what we want and need becomes the center of our attention, we will find ourselves living like a bucket. Jesus sternly warns us about the narcissistic attitude that we are the center of the universe. Again, the parable of the rich farmer is the classic example. The farmer was incredibly successful and had more than his current "bucket" could hold, so he chose to get rid of his smaller bucket and get a larger bucket so he could hold all the new stuff that he had accumulated. Jesus nails the selfishness of the farmer in Luke 12:15 when He warns, "Beware, and be on your guard against every form of greed; for not even when one has an abundance does his life consist of his possessions."

The farmer's bucket was full and overflowing and he was proud of it, but God was not proud of him.

#3: We can find ourselves living like a bucket when we embrace the belief that filling our bucket is the way to find real happiness.

John D. Rockefeller honestly admitted, "I have made many millions, but they have brought me no happiness." However, we still want to believe the lie that "happy is the man whose bucket is full."

Henry Ford confessed after becoming a multi-millionaire, "I was happier doing a mechanic's job." Yet we still want to believe that "happy is the man whose bucket is full."

Solomon—who was perhaps the richest man to have ever lived— agonized about the futility of his riches in Ecclesiastes 2:11, "When I surveyed all that my hands had done and what I had toiled to achieve, everything was meaningless, a chasing after the wind; nothing was gained under the sun" (niv). But we still want to believe that "happy is the man whose bucket is full."

Solomon observed in Ecclesiastes 5:13 what happens when people try to keep what is in their bucket for their own selfish enjoyment, "I have seen a grievous evil under the sun: wealth hoarded to the harm of the owner" (niv).

The Way of the Pipe

I think we can agree that even though our sinful, fallen nature entices us to live life like we are a bucket, it is a cruel fantasy that ultimately leads to disappointment, destruction, and death. But what about living like a pipe? Let us consider this alternative.

#1: We will find ourselves living like a pipe when we understand God created us to be a pipe and not a bucket.

In God's economy, a pipe is infinitely more useful to Him than a bucket! He created us to be conduits and not receptacles of His blessings. In fact, let me ask you, "What happens if a pipe gets confused and starts thinking it is a bucket?" What is supposed to pass through gets stuck, becoming clogged and in need of being roto-rooted—so it can go back to doing what it was made to do—which is to let things flow through it, not just to it.

Do you know what happens to the body when its arteries get clogged up? Or, what a problem it is for the body when your colon gets clogged up? When your internal plumbing is not working, your body is going to be greatly hindered in its normal activities.

God has created many of us to be high-capacity pipes because he wants to pump huge amounts through us to support Kingdom causes worldwide. Let us look at what Paul tells Timothy in 1 Timothy 6:17-19,

Instruct those who are rich in this present world (high capacity pipes) not to be conceited or to fix their hope on the uncertainty of riches, but on God, who richly supplies us with all things to enjoy. Instruct them to do good, to be rich in good works, to be generous and ready to share (let it flow freely), storing up for themselves the treasure of a good foundation for the future, so that they may take hold of that which is life indeed.

Nothing produces "life indeed" like doing what God has created us to do. God has positioned us to turn on our spigot and let it flow!

As R. G. Letourneau said when asked how he could be giving ninety percent of his income away each year and yet still be getting richer. He smiled and confessed. "I keep shoveling it out and God keeps shoveling it right back in—and He has a bigger shovel!"

#2: We will find ourselves living like a pipe when we really believe that what we are letting flow through us today will ultimately flow back to us later.

This is the great eternal "payback" for being a pipe. The bucket gets what it gets while it is here and that is its reward. But the pipe receives a different payback. All that has flowed through it for all those years of life are being recorded and it will all be waiting for us when we relocate to our permanent residence. Malachi 3:16 says, "A book of remembrance was written before Him for those who fear the Lord and who esteem His name." God is monitoring your out-flow.

Jesus assures us of this eternal "payback" in multiple places. In Matthew 6:20-21, He encourages us, "But store up for yourselves treasures in heaven, where neither moth nor rust destroys, and where thieves do not break in or steal; for where your treasure is, there your heart will be also." We lay up for ourselves treasures in heaven by what we willingly divest ourselves of in giving to others in this life.

And again as we saw in Matthew 19:21, Jesus charged the rich, young ruler, "If you wish to be complete, go and sell your possessions and give to the poor, and you will have treasure in heaven; and come, follow Me." Pass it through now and it will be waiting for you in heaven. Jesus was not asking him to give it up; he was just asking him to send it on ahead for later use and enjoyment. Not a bad deal if we keep in mind that this life may last eighty years and eternity, well, it is a lot longer than that!

GIVING FREELY

#3: We will find ourselves living like a pipe when the desires of God's heart truly become the desires of our heart.

Psalm 37:4 is a very powerful verse, "Delight yourself in the Lord; And He will give you the desires of your heart."

Most people have incorrectly interpreted this verse to say, "You delight yourself in the Lord and then the Lord will give you what you want," but it more accurately should be understood this way: "Delight yourself in the Lord and then the Lord will give you His desires for your heart." In other words, as we delight ourselves in Him, He will replace our heart's desires with His heart's desires, so that we will love what He loves and we will hate what He hates. That way we will have compassion on whom He has compassion.

And once God has our heart's desires aligned with His heart's desires, we will find ourselves driven to be a high-capacity pipe allowing as much grace and blessing as possible to fall upon those whom the Lord wants to touch and care for.

We must not forget the sobering words of our Lord who said, "From everyone who has been given much (high-flow capacity), much (high-flow capacity) will be required" (Luke 12:48b).

Jim Elliot, who was martyred trying to share Christ with a native tribe in South America, wrote, "He is no fool who gives what he cannot keep, to gain what he cannot lose." What we accumulate on this earth we cannot keep and what we accumulate in heaven we cannot lose. Seems like a "no brainer," does it not?

May I encourage those of you who God has blessed to be high-capacity pipes to freely open your spigot and let God's blessings and provision pour forth on those who need a blessing from God! If we do, we will have everything to gain and nothing to lose.

FOOD FOR THOUGHT

1. When you reflect on how you are currently living your life, do you see more similarities to living like a bucket or living like a pipe? Why do you think that is the case?

2. What is your greatest personal struggle with the idea of consistently living like a pipe instead of a bucket?

3. In what ways might there be an inconsistency between what Jim Elliott said ("He is no fool who gives what he cannot keep, to gain what he cannot lose.") and how you are currently living your Christian life?

CHAPTER TWELVE

When Giving Got Out of Control

If you want some excellent examples of generous giving, you need only look in the Bible itself. In two different passages we witness some extraordinary and compelling giving stories. One is in the Old Testament and the other is in the New Testament. One involved people who were rich, and the other involved people who were poor. One was for a building program and the other was for benevolent needs. Quite a contrast in many ways, but the outcome in both stories was identical – their giving got out of control.

In the first out-of-control story Moses has come down from Mt. Sinai, his face literally aglow, and reports to the children of Israel that God wants them to build a tabernacle for Him to dwell in. It is important to keep in mind that even though the Israelites were slaves in Egypt for centuries, when they did finally leave that country, they left incredibly wealthy. (See Exodus 12:35-36).

In the second out-of-control story the Macedonian Christians are in the midst of enduring both extended and extreme poverty – themselves barely surviving. Yet, they hear from Paul that the Christians in Jerusalem are facing even more desperate conditions than they are.

Here is Out-of-Control Story #1

(Exodus 35:20-36:7) Then all the congregation of the sons of Israel departed from Moses' presence. Everyone whose heart stirred him and everyone whose spirit moved him came and brought the Lord's contribution for the work of the tent of meeting and for all its service and for the holy garments.

Then all whose hearts moved them, both men and women, came and brought brooches and earrings and signet rings and bracelets, all articles of gold; so did every man who presented an offering of gold to the Lord. Every man, who had in his possession blue and purple and scarlet material and fine linen and goats' hair and rams' skins dyed red and porpoise skins, brought them.

Everyone who could make a contribution of silver and bronze brought the Lord's contribution; and every man who had in his possession acacia wood for any work of the service brought it. All the skilled women spun with their hands, and brought what they had spun, in blue and purple and scarlet material and in fine linen. All the women whose heart stirred with a skill spun the goats' hair.

The rulers brought the onyx stones and the stones for setting for the ephod and for the breastpiece; and the spice and the oil for the light and for the anointing oil and for the fragrant incense. The Israelites, all the men and women, whose heart moved them to bring material for all the work, which the Lord had commanded through Moses to be done, brought a freewill offering to the Lord.

Then Moses said to the sons of Israel, "See, the Lord has called by name Bezalel the son of Uri, the son of Hur, of the tribe of Judah. And He has filled him with the Spirit of God, in wisdom, in understanding and in knowledge and in all craftsmanship; to make designs for working in gold and in silver and in bronze, and in the cutting of stones for settings and in the carving of wood, so as to perform in every inventive work.

He also has put in his heart to teach, both he and Oholiab, of the tribe of Dan. He has filled them with skill to perform every work of an engraver and of a designer and of an embroiderer, in blue and in purple and in scarlet material, and in fine linen, and of a weaver, as performers of every work and makers of designs."

Now (they) and every skillful person in whom the Lord has put skill and understanding to know how to perform all the work in the construction of the sanctuary, shall perform in accordance with all that the Lord has commanded. Then Moses called every skillful person in whom the Lord had put skill, everyone whose heart stirred him, to come to the work to perform it. They received from Moses all the contributions which the sons of Israel had brought to perform the work in the construction of the sanctuary.

And they still continued bringing to him freewill offerings every morning. And all the skillful men who were performing all the work of the sanctuary came, each from the work which he was performing, and they said to Moses, "The people are bringing much more than enough for the construction work which the Lord commanded us to perform."

Then Moses gave an order and they sent this word throughout the camp: "No man or woman is to make anything else as an offering for the sanctuary." And so the people were restrained from bringing more, because what they already had was more than enough to do all the work.

Here is Out-of-Control Story #2

(II Corinthians 8:1-5), "And now, brothers, we want you to know about the grace that God has given the Macedonian churches. Out of the most severe trial, their overflowing joy and their extreme poverty welled up in rich generosity. For I testify that they gave as much as they were able, and even beyond their ability. Entirely on their own, they urgently pleaded with us for the privilege of sharing in this service to the saints. And they did not do as we expected, but they gave themselves first to the Lord and then to us in keeping with God's will."

These two stories are extraordinary examples of what happens when God's people get out of control in their motivation to give. I think it would be quite instructive for us to go behind this explosion of generosity to determine what prompted this kind of out-of-control giving in these two circumstances. I have identified four lessons we can learn from these two stories.

Lesson #1:

Giving will get out of control when <u>God's people catch a bigger vision</u>

Both these visions for doing something greater than themselves began with strong leaders who had a clear vision and were able to effectively articulate that vision and the plan to achieve it – Moses had the blueprints for the tabernacle and Paul intended to personally deliver the benevolent support to the believers in Jerusalem.

I think Will Rogers understood the need for a good plan to accompany a good vision when he stated, "A vision without a plan is a hallucination." Or, as the old proverb says, "A vision without a plan is just a dream. A plan without a vision is just drudgery. But a vision with a plan can change the world." Both leaders had a vision and a plan.

I have a friend who repeats often, "You're getting what you're getting because you're doing what you're doing." In other words more of the same leads to more of the same. This is where most believers find themselves in their giving journeys.

In both these stories, God's people were challenged to embrace a vision that was substantially bigger and more challenging than anything they could envision themselves and they embraced the vision and exceeded all expectation in supporting it as a result.

Lesson #2:

Giving will get out of control when <u>God's people surrender themselves to the Lord</u>

The most obvious statement of this lesson is when Paul says that the Macedonians first gave themselves to the Lord. The beginning of any outbreak of generosity will begin when God's people surrender to Him.

I use the word surrender and not submit for good reason. To submit means to give in. We submit to the authorities over us (government, employers, husbands, etc.) not necessarily because we like what they are doing or agree with their actions, but because we are commanded to submit – to give in – to respectfully yield.

Surrender, on the other hand, is to give up. In this case, there is no objection, no resistance, no biting our lip, no holding our tongue and reluctantly obeying. We completely surrender our will, our opinion, and our self-interests. This is what I believe Paul is getting at when he says that the Macedonians first gave themselves to the Lord. They gladly and willingly surrendered what little they had in material possessions to God. They surrendered their personal agenda for what they wanted to do with those possessions (like having another meal) to God's agenda of helping other believers who were even more needy than they were.

When God's people finally and fully surrender (give up) to God instead of just submit (give in) to God out of respect and duty, out-of-control giving will be positioned to happen.

Lesson #3:

Giving will get out of control when <u>God's people attune their hearts to the voice of the Holy Spirit</u>

We see this repeatedly mentioned in the story of the Israelites. It says the spirit moved them, their heart(s) were stirred and the people were filled with the spirit of God.

When God's people tune their "inner radio" to the right frequency – the frequency of God's voice instead of the frequency of this present age, an eruption of generosity is poised to happen.

Sadly, many pastors, ministers, and church leaders have guided their people to look at their calculators to determine their required level of giving instead of directing them to look to the Holy Spirit for His desired level of giving. The former inhibits out-of-control giving.

Paul is quite clear on the basis for Christian giving in II Corinthians 9:7 (just one chapter after his report of the Macedonian's out-of-control giving). He says, "Each one should do as God has purposed in his heart…" Here Paul is offering us a procedure for determining our giving and not a percentage for determining our giving. He is telling us to tune into the guidance of the Holy Spirit who can stir and move our hearts and fill us with an eagerness to give at levels far beyond anything we have experienced previously.

Lesson #4:

Giving will get out of control when <u>God's people experience joy in giving</u>

Both stories abound with comments about the extraordinary levels of joy His people experienced as their giving got out of control. They had overflowing joy. The people were bringing much more than enough. They were restrained from bringing more. They urgently pleaded for the privilege of sharing. They gave beyond their ability.

Wouldn't you love to be part of a worship service one day where the leaders of the church get up at the offering time and tell the congregation that they are not going to take up an offering because they already have more than enough to perform the work that the church is doing? It would be a modern day manifestation of out-of-control giving.

If you read the rest of II Corinthians 9:7 you will see this fourth lesson emphasized. Paul concludes his giving instructions that we should give, "...not grudgingly, nor under compulsion, for God loves a cheerful giver." The Greek word for "cheerful" could also be translated "hilarious." When the act of giving itself brings us out-of-control joy, out-of-control giving is on the verge of breaking out.

How can we increase our joy in giving? One way would be for when we give to actually be able to see the results of our giving – the lives that will be changed or the work that will be done. I have heard of surveys that indicate that of all the giving that Christians do, church giving gives them the least amount of joy. One reason is because the church has done such an inadequate job of connecting their members to the impact their weekly giving is having in the lives of people locally and internationally. Their giving simply goes in the plate, never to be seen or heard about again. Yet, these same folks derive great joy in supporting a needy child in a third-world country. Why? It is because they are connected to the recipient and to the outcome.

Wouldn't it be inspiring if each week just prior to the offering, your church would show a short one minute video of someone who has been impacted by the ministry of your church – a person who got saved – a marriage that was rescued – someone who was helped to overcome an addiction – a child who was impacted by a VBS program – a tribe in a foreign country that now has the Word of God in their language, etc. because of the ministry of the church? You could call this little video vignette the "Money Clip." Wouldn't that make giving more meaningful and much more joyous for everyone?

Connecting giving to specific outcomes opens the door for greatly increased joy in giving. And the more "hilarious" we become in our giving the more likely we are to start giving like the Israelites in Exodus 35-36 and the Macedonians in II Corinthians 8.

If you want to experience out-of-control giving, (1.) embrace a bigger vision, (2.) totally surrender to the Lord, (3.) listen to the Holy Spirit, and (4.) make your giving a joyous experience. Then, look out!

FOOD FOR THOUGHT

1. Why do you think "surrender" is a requirement for out-of-control giving?

2. What has been the most personally meaningful (joy-filled) gift you have ever made and why was it so?

3. What have been the times in your life where you think you may have gotten more of a blessing out of your giving than the receiver did?

CHAPTER THIRTEEN

For Richer or For Poorer

We most often hear this phrase, "for richer or for poorer" in wedding vows, but I believe this phrase may also be used to describe a core issue for us in regards to our giving. Let me explain. I have observed over the years that one of the most compelling disincentives to people's giving is a nagging sense of loss from what they give away. Many feel that if they give, they will become "poorer" in the same proportion as the recipient of their gift becomes "richer." In other words, "Someone else's gain is at my expense." So, they think, "I need to evaluate how much I can afford to lose in my giving – how much poorer I am willing to become – in order to determine how much I am willing to give."

May I suggest that this kind of thinking, common as it is, is the absolute opposite of what the Word of God teaches us about giving. The Bible unquestionably teaches us that our giving is never a personal loss. It is always a personal gain. In fact, I hope to convince you that it is impossible for any of us to divest ourselves of our acquired wealth by giving it away to bless and serve others.

Let me begin by first asking you a simple question. When you put money into your retirement plan or make a principal payment on your home mortgage loan, do you feel poorer in so doing? I think not. We understand that we have simply transferred these funds to a different asset that is not immediately useful, but will ultimately be very beneficial to us in the future. I would go so far as to say that in making these transfers we actually feel better off financially and even more secure by doing so, even though our net worth statement has not changed at all in the transfer.

There is a repeated phrase in the New Testament that I believe most of us have not carefully considered. The phrase "Lay up treasure(s)" is used in Matthew 6:20, Luke 12:20 and I Timothy 6:19. It is interesting that the Greek word for "lay up" is related to the root word for "treasure." So, you could literally translate the phrase, "treasure up treasures." We read, for example, in Matthew 6:20 that we are to be "lay(ing) up treasures in heaven."

What seems to have escaped our notice is the two other words that are in the middle of this phrase - "for yourselves." Jesus says, "lay up treasures for yourselves in heaven." These treasures are not being laid up in heaven for God, or for the poor or for the lost. We are laying them up for ourselves. We are not losing them, we are simply transferring readily liquid and immediately available assets into an account that is not immediately liquid nor readily available, but will be of great value to us in the future. And every gift (transfer) we make in this life is being credited to our account in heaven – every one of them, no matter how great or how small.

In I Timothy 6:17-19, Paul reiterates this same idea when he is writing to Timothy about the affluent Christians under his spiritual care. He says, "Command those who are rich in this present world not to be arrogant nor to put their hope in wealth, which is so uncertain, but to put their hope in God, who richly provides us with everything for our enjoyment. Command them to do good, to be rich in good deeds, and to be generous and willing to share. In this way they will lay up treasure for themselves as a firm foundation for the coming age, so that they may take hold of that which is life indeed."

These affluent Christians are not being commanded to divest themselves of their material treasures, they are being commanded to lay up their treasures for themselves – for later enjoyment – "for the coming age" – an eternal retirement plan or equity position.

The rich farmer is called a "fool" in Luke 12:20 because he was mistakenly "laying up treasures for himself" here on earth. He was properly investing for himself, only he was doing it in an improper place! (See Matthew 6:19.)

Let me even go so far as to say that we cannot give anything away that we possess. We can at best only lay it up in a different account. But in the end, no matter where we give it, it has been credited to our heavenly balance sheet and it will make us ultimately (and sometimes even immediately) richer than before we made the transfer. Add to this fact that when we lay up (invest) treasures for ourselves in Kingdom things, God's return on that investment is always guaranteed - never a downturn in God's economy. Remember, investing in the Kingdom for the King always makes you richer – never poorer.

Let me give you just a few additional scriptures that further confirm the immediate and ultimate profitability of laying up treasures for yourselves in heavenly things.

We read in Acts 20:35, "In all things I have shown you that by working hard in this way we must help the weak and remember the words of the Lord Jesus, how he himself said, 'It is more blessed to give than to receive.'" We gain.

Proverbs 11:25 tells us, "A generous man will prosper; he who refreshes others will himself be refreshed." We gain.

In Luke 6:38, Jesus encourages us, "Give, and it will be given to you. A good measure, pressed down, shaken together and running over, will be poured into your lap. For with the measure you use, it will be measured to you." We gain.

We can see in these verses that we are not just richer financially, but also emotionally because our giving refreshes us as well as those we give to; spiritually because our giving more perfectly conforms us into the image of Christ – the ultimate giver; and relationally because not only do we profit from our investment, others profit as well – a double blessing.

I am reminded of the young boy who gave Jesus what was no doubt a hearty lunch of five loaves and two fishes (Matthew 14:13, Mark 6:33, Luke 9:12, John 6:1). (This story is one of a very few that is actually reported in all four gospels. It obviously made a huge impression on everyone.) I am confident when the boy gave his sack of food to Jesus he thought he was giving up his lunch – a loss. But he was okay with that. After all, it was for Jesus. Little did he know that not only would he still have his lunch, but thousands of others would also have lunch thanks to him. Having once been a young boy myself, I imagine this lad likely ended up eating more than his original five loaves and two fish before the day was done. He wasn't poorer because of his gift, he was actually richer and so were all those who were with him. No loss.

Anne Frank, the young Jewish girl who was eventually killed in a Nazi concentration camp wrote, "No one has ever become poor by giving." Do you know why? Because you cannot become poor by giving. It is an eternal impossibility.

Do you see yourself as being poorer after you write the check or make the gift? Do you feel like you have lost and someone else has gained?

Do you sense that you are worse off than you were before you gave? Perish the thought! You are richer! You have just laid up for yourself more treasures in heaven. You are now more blessed and your future more secure than before. You have willingly transferred some readily available, immediately liquid assets to another account that will be waiting for you when you finally "retire" from this life and move on to the next one – the best one. And in that day you will be glad you invested so generously with a long view of life and eternity. Someday, oh, happy day, all our invested treasures will finally be returned to us to use and to enjoy - forever!

FOOD FOR THOUGHT

1. Think about the statement, "We cannot give anything away that we possess." How will this change your thinking about giving knowing that if we give it away, we get it back later?

2. Anne Frank said, "You cannot become poor by giving." Consider this idea. Can you think of a time in your life where the fear of not having enough for yourself kept you from giving generously?

3. How will this understanding of being rewarded for what you give of yourself and the resources you have been entrusted with change your attitude and your motivation to give?

Okay, I have completed this first leg of my life stewardship journey, where do I go from here?

Want to get your entire church involved?

An expansion of these life stewardship concepts in this book are available in multiple small group formats.

- Digital Format: Multiple 6 lesson video based study modules (graded from most basic to most challenging)
- Digital Format: 6 session Pastors and Church Leaders video module
- DVD format: 13 week DVD based study

The content of this study will challenge and stretch both your most mature believers as well as your newest Christians. This study has the capability to deeply impact a broad range of believers regardless of their level of maturity.

Visit www.stewardshipministries.org

THE ONE QUESTION

THAT CHANGES EVERYTHING

A SIX WEEK LIFE STEWARDSHIP STUDY

HIGH SCHOOL

The high school curriculum is an adapted version of the adult life stewardship series. The objective of this curriculum is for students to have an age-appropriate understanding of the concept of life stewardship and to learn how to begin effectively implementing that understanding into various areas of their lives.

Lesson #1   One Question

Asking the One Question that Changes Everything: The Concept of a Steward

Lesson #2   Your Place In The World

Understanding Who You Are: The Worldview of a Steward

Lesson #3   What's Mine is Yours

Living the Generous Life: The Lifestyle of a Steward

Lesson #4   Three Rings

Discovering Your Fire Within: The Life Purpose of a Steward

Lesson #5   A Balancing Act

Choosing the Company You Keep: The Relationships of a Steward

Lesson #6   Don't Forget

Remembering Who You Belong To: The Mindset of a Steward

THE ONE QUESTION THAT CHANGES EVERYTHING

JUNIOR HIGH

During the early teen years, students are moldable, yet incredibly susceptible to the material world around them. The objective of this curriculum is for students to have an age-appropriate understanding of the concept of life stewardship and to learn how to begin effectively implementing that understanding into various areas of their lives.

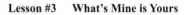

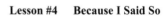

Lesson #1   God Owns Everything

Asking the One Question that Changes Everything: The Concept of a Steward

Lesson #2   When I Grow Up

Discovering Why You Were Created: The Life Purpose of a Steward

Lesson #3   What's Mine is Yours

Living the Generous Life: The Lifestyle of a Steward

Lesson #4   Because I Said So

Understanding Authority: The Submission of a Steward

Lesson #5   Better Together

Establishing Good Friends: The Relationships of a Steward

Lesson #6   Don't Forget

Remembering Who You Belong To: The Mindset of a Steward

Life Stewardship Curriculum for Children

Cruising on the USS Stewardship

NEW!

If you are looking for both powerful and unique content to begin discipling even your youngest children in life stewardship principles and practices, this children's life stewardship curriculum is exactly what you are looking for.

Cruising on the USS Stewardship Part 1

Lesson #1   Charting the Course | Kick-Off!

Lesson #2   The Parable of the Talents
(Understanding what stewardship means)

Lesson #3   God's Great Creation
(Understanding that God created all things and is the owner of all things)

Lesson #4   God's Purpose For Us
(Understanding that God has a place and purpose for each of us)

Lesson #5   The Widow's Mite
(Understanding that giving is an expression of worship to God)

Lesson #6   Zacchaeus Changes His Lifestyle
(Understanding that God wants us to live an honoring lifestyle)

Cruising on the USS Stewardship Part 2

Lesson #1   The Good Samaritan
(Understanding that God wants us to share our blessings with others)

Lesson #2   Nehemiah Rebuilds the Wall
(Understanding that God cares about us and we need to listen to him)

Lesson #3   King Solomon Builds a Temple
(Understanding that we need to be thankful for our church and help care for it.)

Lesson #4   Give to Caesar What Belongs to Caesar
(Understanding what we have belongs to God and we should give extravagantly)

Lesson #5   Don't Forget Who You Belong To
(Understanding the many ways in which we belong to God)

Lesson #6   Docking Celebration!

Now Available!

Pastors and Church Leaders Life Stewardship Study

A church will never be able to develop a church-wide life stewardship culture if the leadership of the church does not understand, personally practice and effectively teach and preach these principles themselves.

To order this and other life stewardship resources, visit stewardshipministries.org